OLLEGE LIBRARY

The Story of

Noah
and the Ark

For all the children who helped me write this story — M. McC.

For my niece Erika — G. F.

Barefoot Books
124 Walcot Street
Bath
BA1 5BG

This book was typeset in Novarese Medium 18pt on 26pt leading
The illustrations were prepared in watercolours and coloured pencils on watercolour paper

Graphic design by designsection, Frome
Colour separation by Grafiscan, Verona
Printed and bound in Singapore by Tien Wah Press (Pte) Ltd

This book has been printed on 100% acid-free paper

Hardcover ISBN 1 84148 360 5
Paperback ISBN 1 84148 362 1

British Cataloguing-in-Publication Data: a catalogue
record for this book is available from the British Library

3 5 7 9 8 6 4

The Story of

Noah
and the Ark

retold by Michael McCarthy

illustrated by Giuliano Ferri

Barefoot Books
Celebrating Art and Story

God made the world all fresh and new,
Each tree, and field, and hill.
But folks were not like me and you,
They learned to fight and kill.

The world was soon so stained with blood
That God was very sad.
God thought, 'I'll send a mighty flood
To wash out all things bad.'

But God's friend Noah was kind and good,
So were all his family.
They helped each other as they should
And loved each other dearly.

God said, 'The good must never drown.
I must keep them alive.
I'll put in place a special plan
To help them all survive.'

God said to Noah, 'Build an ark',
Then told him what to do.
Noah listened, made a mark,
With each line straight and true.

He built the Ark of Cypress wood.
There were three decks inside it.
Sealed with pitch from toe to head,
It stretched three hundred cubits.

Noah worked as God had said:
The Ark was stout and strong.
Soon it towered overhead,
This tall, this wide, this long.

Cows and horses, dogs and cats,
Camels, reindeer, donkeys,
Foxes, badgers, mice and rats,
Tigers, lions, monkeys.

Birds as well from all the seas,
Birds from all the hills.
Parrots, finches, hummingbirds,
Gulls and razorbills.

Crocodiles and chimpanzees,
Lizards, snails and slugs;
Centipedes and bumble-bees,
Butterflies and bugs.

Two of each climbed in the Ark,
Until the evening sky grew dark.
Then Noah shut and locked the door,
And waited for the rain to pour.

The birds preferred to perch up high,
For eagles want to see the sky.
The reptiles slithered down below,
Where they could hear the water flow.

Said the giraffes: 'If no one cares,
We'd like to sit beside the stairs.
There's lots of room to stretch our necks.'
Elephants took the middle decks.

Then came Mister Rain.

He poured for forty days and nights
With a dark and fearful frown.
He filled each living thing with fright,
For they knew that they would drown.

He raged around the rocks and crags,
With torrents, floods and fountains.
He rose above the highest hills,
And covered all the mountains.

At last, one day God called out loud,
'Mrs Wind! Remove the clouds!'
She blew so much it's not surprising
The waters of the flood stopped rising.

For five long months the waters dropped,
The Ark still floating on the top.
At last it touched, and then it sat
Upon the Mount of Ararat.

'Now,' Noah said, 'we'll find a haven.'
To start the search, he called a raven.
She flew up high and looked around.
She saw no sign of solid ground.

Next day, a dove flew east and west,
But could not find a place to rest.
So Noah waited one more week
Then thought he'd take another peek.

He sent the dove across the sea.
She found herself an olive tree.
She brought a twig back straight away,
And Noah shouted out, 'Hurray!'

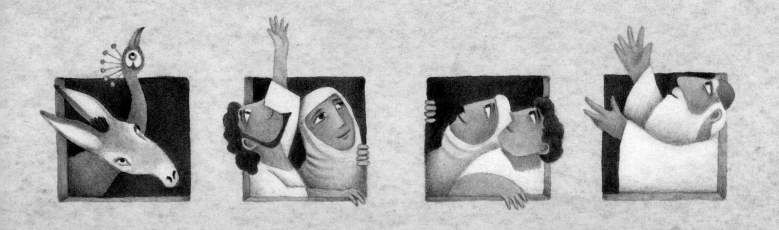

After so long inside the Ark,
The time had come to disembark.

All the creatures called goodbye,
And ran outside to see the sky.

Noah himself at last climbed out,
And all his family gave a shout.
They built an altar where they prayed,
And then an offering was made.

God enjoyed its fragrant smell
And said to Noah, 'Listen well.
I promise, after so much pain,
A flood will never come again.

Go out from here and multiply.
Let creatures fill the earth and sky.
All things that swim or breathe the air
Will be forever in your care.'

Next God took all the colours seven
To make a rainbow high in heaven;
Then spread it out across the sky,
And we all know the reason why.

For when the sun shines through the rain
The rainbow's arc appears again.
Reminding me, reminding you,
God's words to Noah are still true.

Author's Note

I approached this project on three fronts.

I read several translations of the flood story, among them the Revised Standard version and the New Jerusalem version. I also read various biblical commentaries, such as *The Jerome Biblical Commentary* and *Dictionaries of the Bible* edited by McKenzie and Dufour. I was especially inspired and educated by Robert Alter's new translation, *Genesis*.

At the same time, I made frequent visits to the reception classes at our local school. I spent time with the children, reading and telling stories, and checking their library. Oscar Wilde's stories for children played a central part here, as well as traditional nursery rhymes.

Finally, I laid my hands on as many animal, bird, insect and reptile books as I could find. As I consulted these books, I let my memory take me to the various zoos I have visited in my life.

In the middle of all this, I took a week off and flew to The Gambia, in West Africa, where I visited several wildlife parks and bird sanctuaries.

During my research, I became aware that the Genesis account is a compilation of two flood stories. This eased the task of deciding what to leave in and what to leave out. Robert Alter's *Genesis* was invaluable in demonstrating how the original narrative was compiled, and showing how poetry and 'drum roll' effects were used to heighten the intensity at crucial parts of the tale.

All in all, I wanted to create a story that had the power and magic of the original, and would stretch the vocabulary and imagination of its listeners. I hope that the retelling here will capture the imagination of children of all ages.

Michael McCarthy

Barefoot Books
Celebrating Art and Story

At Barefoot Books, we celebrate art and story with books that open
the hearts and minds of children from all walks of life, inspiring them to read
deeper, search further, and explore their own creative gifts. Taking our
inspiration from many different cultures, we focus on themes that encourage
independence of spirit, enthusiasm for learning, and acceptance of other
traditions. Thoughtfully prepared by writers, artists and storytellers from
all over the world, our products combine the best of the present with the best
of the past to educate our children as the caretakers of tomorrow.

www.barefootbooks.com